OTHER BOOKS BY THIS AUTHOR

The Hamster Revolution

The Hamster Revolution for Meetings

sm

Mike Song

Edited by Rachel Metzger

ZIPs for Outlook, iPad, iPhone, Gmail, Google, and Much, Much More!

BK

Berrett–Koehler Publishers, Inc.
San Francisco
a BK Business book

Berrett-Koehler Publishers, Inc.
235 Montgomery Street, Suite 650
San Francisco, CA 94104-2916
Tel: (415) 288-0260   Fax: (415) 362-2512
www.bkconnection.com

Ordering Information
Quantity sales. Special discounts are available on quantity purchases by corporations, associations, and others. For details, contact the "Special Sales Department" at the Berrett-Koehler address above.

Individual sales. Berrett-Koehler publications are available through most bookstores. They can also be ordered directly from Berrett-Koehler: Tel: (800) 929-2929; Fax: (802) 864-7626; www.bkconnection.com

Orders for college textbook/course adoption use. Please contact Berrett-Koehler: Tel: (800) 929-2929; Fax: (802) 864-7626.

Orders by U.S. trade bookstores and wholesalers. Please contact Ingram Publisher Services, Tel: (800) 509-4887; Fax: (800) 838-1149; E-mail: customer.service@ingrampublisherservices.com; or visit www.ingrampublisherservices.com/Ordering for details about electronic ordering.

Berrett-Koehler and the BK logo are registered trademarks of Berrett-Koehler Publishers, Inc.
Printed in the United States of America

Berrett-Koehler books are printed on long-lasting acid-free paper. When it is available, we choose paper that has been manufactured by environmentally responsible processes. These may include using trees grown in sustainable forests, incorporating recycled paper, minimizing chlorine in bleaching, or recycling the energy produced at the paper mill.

Library of Congress Cataloging-in-Publication Data
Song, Mike, 1964–
    Zip! tips / Mike Song ; edited by Rachel Metzger. — First edition.
      pages cm
    "ZIPs for Outlook, iPad, iPhone, Gmail, Google, and Much, Much More!."
    Includes index.
    ISBN 978-1-60994-915-0 (pbk.)
    1. Personal information management.   2. Information technology—Management.   I. Title.
    HD30.2.S669 2013
    650.1'1—dc23   2013008498

First Edition
18   17   16   15   14   13   10   9   8   7   6   5   4   3   2   1

Cover/Jacket Designer: Pemastudio
Cover Art: Chris Volpe Photography
Interior Design: George Whipple

For Emily, Evan, and Ethan
—You can do it!

CONTENTS

PREFACE

The age of *ZIP!* has arrived and will forever change the way we work and succeed. *ZIP!* is a new business philosophy that takes the view that the fastest way to boost performance is to focus on technology skills versus time management. I developed this idea as a result of analyzing five powerful business trends:

The Tech-Immersion Trend The average knowledge worker now spends more than 80 percent[1] of the day using technologies such as Outlook, the web, IM, iPad, and smartphones. Even meetings are scheduled via e-calendars and are more virtual than ever. As a result, the value of learning tech tips has soared.

The Scratch-the-Surface Trend Today, we're handed a computer, tablet, or phone and are expected to magically master all its features. "Here's your iPad. Good luck!"

---

1. Mike Song, "The Tech Opportunity: How Everyday Tech Skills Can Boost Performance, Productivity, and Profits," GetControl.net/blog, 2013.

Incredibly, 98 percent[2] of busy professionals only discover the most superficial tech features. The most common thing I hear when teaching *ZIP!* Tips is "Wow! I never knew I could do that!"

The Tech-Obsession Trend Let's face it; we're obsessed with our devices. In fact, 80 percent of all professionals get mad at colleagues who pay more attention to their smartphones than to them!

The Use-It-Forever-Everywhere Trend Initially, my publisher worried that new software releases would make this book obsolete. Not so! Most of the Outlook tips, such as creative ways to drag and drop e-mails to convert them into contacts, tasks, and calendar items, have been present in the last five software releases. Also, most *ZIP!* Tips now work on products from many different manufacturers including Microsoft, Apple, and Google. The trend is toward software and advice that lasts and is flexible.

The Time-Crunch Trend We are constantly being asked to do more with less time and resources. This increases the need for short and effective learning experiences and solutions that are quick to learn and easy to use.

I hope you'll join me on an extraordinary journey to a better, smarter, and faster you, who feels more relaxed and in control.

Enjoy your success!

---

2. Ibid.

RELAPSE

Harold Gets Hamsterized

I couldn't believe my eyes. Harold had relapsed! He'd turned back into a two-foot hamster and was pacing to and fro on his little rodent legs, dragging his microsized briefcase behind him.

"You did this to me!" he shouted, pointing a furry finger at me.

Okay, let's back up a bit. I'm a productivity coach, and a few years ago I helped Harold with, um . . . a delicate little problem. He had become so overwhelmed with e-mail, interruptions, and tasks that he'd turned into a hamster. Why a hamster? Because, these days, most professionals are *running in place* at work like hamsters on never-ending, exhausting wheels.

Today, Harold was back, as one very frustrated rodent. He dropped his briefcase and spun toward me.

"Look at me! I'm supposed to be prepping for a huge press conference."

"Press conference?"

"Yes! I've got to address the entire Foster and Schrubb executive team—and the media—*in less than three hours.* We're launching a new customer service app, and I am so far behind! I still need to create handouts, brief my team, polish my speech . . . "

"Wow!" I said. "When did you start feeling so overwhelmed?"

"It started a month ago and . . . yikes!"

Harold stared down at his arms in horror.

"It's getting worse. I'm getting furrier, shorter, and more hamsterish. Good grief!"

As he buried his head in his paws, gasping for breath, I bent down to place a hand on his heaving shoulders.

"Quick, Harold," I urged, "have you changed anything about the way you work since we last spoke?"

Harold's furry brow furrowed as he considered my question.

"Yes! I attended a full-day time-management class exactly one month ago when this all started. They taught me all about daily lists, prioritizing my tasks with four codes, and getting my inbox to zero but . . . somehow, it's only seemed to make me busier and busier."

Aha! I held up my hand.

"I know what's wrong, and I'll explain later," I said urgently. "But right now, we've got to stop the hamsterization process—stat! Harold, you need to discover a powerful new concept called *ZIP!*"

"What's 'zip'?" Harold asked.

"*ZIP!* is lightning in a bottle . . . a hurricane in a can. *ZIP!* is rocket fuel for your career and a spa day for your stressed-out soul!"

Harold rolled his eyes impatiently. "Yeah, and I suppose it does laundry too."

"Not quite," I replied with a smile. "But it's the fastest way to get more done, and *that's* what will turn you back into a human being."

"What on earth are you talking about?"

"*ZIP!* focuses on the fastest-growing and most rapidly changing aspect of our lives: technology. It's a business philosophy that combines core success principles with quick-to-learn, easy-to-use tech tips. I call them *ZIP!* Tips. It's the new cure for overwhelmed business hamsters like you."

"Stop with the infomercial. Give me an example," Harold demanded, peering at me skeptically.

"Okay, here's the first core principle," I said.

 **CORE PRINCIPLE #1**

Tech Management Is the Fastest Way to Get More Done.

"So it's more about tech management than time management?" Harold asked.

"Exactly. And *ZIP!* isn't just about one technology like Outlook or iPhone; it focuses on *all* your software and devices and how they interact with each other. That's—"

"So these *ZIP!* Tips will reverse the hamsterization process?"

"Yes."

"Show me," he insisted, eager to reclaim his humanity.

I scooped him up and popped him onto the chair next to my laptop. Then I paused, looking around the room, as if I were about to reveal a top-secret plan.

"Do you have any long phrases that you need to type every day?"

"Of course," Harold said quickly. "I've got a bunch of them."

"Give me an example."

"Well, I have to type my team name, Foster and Schrubb Organizational Development Team, quite a bit."

I tapped out a quick adjustment on my computer, and then turned the keyboard toward Harold.

"Type in 'fd,'" I said.

Harold hit the two keys and turned to me, exasperated.

"I think you're losing it. Why are we—?"

I put my finger to my lips.

"Shh, it's time to *ZIP!* Now hit the space bar in . . . three, two, one, now!"

Harold nervously tapped the space bar, and I yelled, "Bam!"

On the screen, the entire phrase magically popped out: Foster and Schrubb Organizational Development Team.

"Wow!" Harold cried. "How'd you *do* that? I've been typing those fifty flipping letters for eight years!"

"Never again!" I cried. "From now on, the Amazing AutoCorrector is going to zip out your long phrases in a nanosecond."

Harold began to look hopeful for the first time.

"You gotta show me how you did that magic trick!" he cried.

"It's magic," I said. "The kind that happens when you activate your robots."

 CORE PRINCIPLE #2

Activate Your Robots!

Harold looked perplexed. "Robots? Like C3PO? I don't have any robots."

"Yes you do, Harold," I explained. "In order to *ZIP!*, you must change the way you think about technology. You have a whole *fleet* of useful robots, but they're gathering robot dust in their lonely robot corners."

"Are you crazy? Where are they?" Harold asked, looking around nervously.

"They live *inside* your technology. You see, Harold, the robots are here, at your fingertips!"

"So you're saying that the robots that we've been waiting for, the ones that would help us with all kinds of tough tasks, have been right here all along, in our computers?"

"Exactly." I smiled. "And Harold, you just met your first robot."

"Wow!" Harold marveled. "So what's next?"

"First, I need to share a little secret with you."

THE AMAZING AUTOCORRECTOR

Type Long Phrases in a Flash

I paused for a moment to gaze out the window, taking a deep breath. Storm clouds were gathering on the horizon. Harold's visit confirmed what I had suspected: the dark forces of chaos and overwhelm were gathering strength, turning more and more professionals like Harold into hamsters.

It was time for hamsters everywhere to fight back. The moment had finally come.

I turned from the window, grabbed at hidden Velcro ties, and dramatically tore away my business suit. I stood tall and proud—fists on hips—in my shiny, new, black-and-orange superhero costume, a bold, blue Z emblazoned on my chest.

"I am Z!" I cried out mightily, complete with a neat echoing sound effect.

I'm pretty sure beams of light emanated from my very aura.

Harold's jaw dropped, and he fell off his chair.

"The *ZIP!* Tips I'll share will help you and millions of others become productivity superheroes!"

Now over his initial shock, Harold burst out laughing.

"Productivity superheroes? Are you nuts? I'd be happy just to be human again."

"Understood," I said with a smile. "I know it sounds crazy, but I'm asking you to believe that you are about to gain some superhuman skills. Do you trust me?"

Harold glanced down at his furry arms and sighed. "Do I have a choice? It sounds like *ZIP!* Tips are my only hope."

"You're not alone," I said, glancing at the dark clouds rolling toward us.

"Z, you look ridiculous," Harold said. "No offense."

"None taken," I replied, making a mental note to speak with my tailor.

I reached into a secret compartment in my desk and reverently produced a small, black book titled, *Top-Secret ZIP! Tips*. The book seemed to glow a little, and Harold looked at it in awe.

"Are you ready to *ZIP!*?"

"Let's do it," Harold said.

"Okay, open up your laptop and launch Outlook!" I cried. "I'm going to show you how to use the Amazing AutoCorrector."

"Will this robot *only* work in the latest version of Outlook?" Harold asked, as he pulled his laptop out of his briefcase.

"No. That's another core principle of *ZIP!*"

 **CORE PRINCIPLE #3**

> ### The Best ZIP! Tips Work Forever and Everywhere.

"This *ZIP!* Tip has worked on the last four versions of Outlook and it works for PC, Mac, iPhone, BlackBerry, and iPad users too. You can also use it in Word, Excel, PowerPoint, and OneNote!"

"Wow!" Harold said. "I can use this one *ZIP!* Tip in a zillion places. I could even help colleagues and friends who use different technologies."

"Exactamundo!" I replied. "Let's get started with your PC version of Outlook first. The trick is to use Outlook's AutoCorrect function to trigger longer phrases when you type a two letter code."

I opened the *ZIP!* Tips book to the right page and handed it to Harold. He smiled.

"These are simple steps, let me try . . ."

"One more thing," I added. "When you see italics in the instructions, it means that that word or phrase is a menu item that you need to tap."

Harold nodded and began to implement his first Amazing AutoCorrect.

ROBOT: THE AMAZING AUTOCORRECTOR

JOB: Saves time by typing long, commonly used phrases with a few keystrokes.

The Amazing AutoCorrector for Outlook 2003, 2007, 2010, and 2013 (PC Version)

First, surf to the special menu page where you can program your time-saving Amazing AutoCorrectors. Here are the directions:

- **For Outlook 2003:** Click on *Tools > Options > Spelling > AutoCorrect Options* to arrive at the AutoCorrect programming page, also known as the trigger page. Type a short trigger phrase in the *Replace* box and your commonly used, longer phrase in the *With* box. Click on *Add* and *OK*. Then open a new e-mail, type the trigger phrase, and tap the space bar.

- **For Outlook 2007:** Click on *Tools > Options > Spelling and Autocorrect > AutoCorrect Options* to arrive at the AutoCorrect programming page, also known as the trigger page. Type a short trigger phrase in the *Replace* box and your longer phrase in the *With* box. Click on *Add* and *OK*. Then, open a new e-mail, type the trigger phrase, and tap the space bar.

- **For Outlook 2010 and 2013:** Click on *File > Options > Mail > Spelling and Autocorrect > AutoCorrect Options* to arrive at the AutoCorrect programming page, also known as the trigger page. Type a short trigger phrase in the *Replace* box and your longer phrase in the *With* box. Click on *Add* and *OK*. Then, open a new e-mail, type the trigger phrase, and tap the spacebar.

  Example: Replace a short phrase such as "zt" with your commonly used, longer phrase such as "*ZIP!* Tips: the Fastest Way to Get More Done."

The Amazing AutoCorrector for Microsoft Word, Excel, PowerPoint, and OneNote 2007

- For 2007 versions, click on the Windows Office button in upper-left corner and then *Word*, *Excel*, *PowerPoint*, or *OneNote Options > Proofing > AutoCorrect Options*.

- Type a short trigger phrase in the *Replace* box and your longer phrase in the *With* box.

    Example: Replace "zt" with "*ZIP!* Tips: the Fastest Way to Get More Done."

- Click on *Add* and *OK*.

The Amazing AutoCorrector for Microsoft Word, Excel, PowerPoint, and OneNote 2010 and 2013

- For 2010 and 2013 versions, click on *File* > *Options* > *Proofing* > *AutoCorrect Options*.
- Type a short trigger phrase in the *Replace* box and your longer phrase in the *With* box.

    Example: Replace "zt" with "*ZIP!* Tips: the Fastest Way to Get More Done."

- Click on *Add* and *OK*.

The Amazing AutoCorrector for Mac Mail and MAC Outlook 2011

(It's called "Text Replacement." Amazing AutoCorrectors transfer between Mac Mail and Outlook 2011, Mac Notes, and Mac Calendar.)

- Open Mac Mail and open a new e-mail.
- Move your mouse to the top of the screen to reveal the topmost menu.
- Select *Edit* > *Substitutions*.
- Make sure that *Text Replacement* is checked.
- From the same menu, select *Show Substitutions*.

- Click on *Text Preferences* and + to add a new Auto-Correct.
- Type a short trigger phrase in the *Replace* box and your longer phrase in the *With box* and tap *Enter*.
- **Bonus *ZIP!* Tip:** Your amazing AutoCorrects will also work in Mac Notes and in the calendar.

The Amazing AutoCorrector for Mac Word, PowerPoint, and Excel 2011

- Open Mac Word, PowerPoint, or Excel and move your mouse to the top of the screen to reveal the drop-down menu.
- Select *Tools* > *AutoCorrect*.
- Type a short trigger phrase in the *Replace* box and your longer phrase in the *With* box.
- Click on *Add* to save.
- **Bonus *ZIP!* Tip:** In many cases, the AutoCorrects you create will transfer from Word to Excel and PowerPoint.

The Amazing AutoCorrector for iPhone and iPad

(It's called "Shortcuts.")

- Go to *Settings* > *General* > *Keyboard* and tap *Shortcuts*.
- Tap *Add New Shortcut* to arrive at the AutoCorrect programming page, also known as the trigger page.
- Type the longer phrase in the *Phrase* box.
- Type the short trigger phrase in the *Shortcut* box and tap *Save*.

The Amazing AutoCorrector for BlackBerry

(It's called "Word Substitution" on most BlackBerry smart-phones.)

- Tap *All* from your main window.
- Tap *Options*. (It's an icon that looks like a wrench.)
- Tap *Typing* and *Input > Word Substitution*.
  (Readers with older software versions may need to go to *Options > AutoText* instead of *Input > Word Substitution*.)
- Tap the menu button, which is to the left of the center track pad and has seven dots on it.
- Tap *New* to arrive at the *AutoCorrect* programming page, also known as the trigger page.
- Type your short trigger phrase under the word *Replace*.
- Type your longer phrase under the word *With*.

Once Harold was done, he opened a new e-mail, typed "ss," tapped the space bar, and out popped: Foster and Schrubb Job Satisfaction Survey.

"Yes!" he cried, jumping up and down on the chair, fist-pumping—or, paw-pumping. "I did it!"

I felt a jolt of positive energy run through my body. I love helping others get more done.

"Amazing," Harold said. "You just saved me about 500 keystrokes a day."

I jabbed at my iPhone's calculator and replied, "With 245 annual work days, that cuts 122,500 key strokes a year!"

"This is going to change the world!" Harold murmured, stunned. "Our company has 10,000 employees, so this one *ZIP!* Tip would save us . . ."

"1.2 billion keystrokes per year!" I blurted out, holding up my iPhone. "That's billion with a *b*."

Harold was speechless.

"More great news," I said. "These Amazing AutoCorrectors transfer automatically to Word, Excel, and other Office programs, like magic."

"That *doubles* the keystrokes I'm going to save," Harold squeaked giddily. "If my whole company uses this tip, we'll save more than 2.4 billion clicks a year."

"It's all about tech management," I reminded him.

"Not time management. I get it!" Harold cried. He was nearly jumping out of his fur. "Save time, boost performance, better life balance—*ZIP!*"

"You mentioned your company," I added. "You might be interested in sharing my free *ZIP!* Tips class at Zip-Tips.com with your colleagues. It's packed with fast, fun videos. So, you can teach the Amazing AutoCorrector to your whole company for free!"

The *ZIP!* Tips Class

Go to Zip-Tips.com and I'll guide you through the entire process. You'll need this top-secret enrollment key to prove you are a true member of the *ZIP!* revolution.

Top-Secret Reader Enrollment Key: zipnow

Questions? Call 888-340-3598
or visit: Zip-Tips.com/info

Harold's head was clearly spinning. "My team is going to love this! What's next, Z?"

THE DRAFTINATOR

Easy Templates You Can Insert Fast

"There are many more robots in your fleet, Harold," I said.

"I love the Amazing AutoCorrector robot. But is there a robot that could pop larger, preformatted paragraphs or snippets of text into e-mail and documents for me?"

"Yes. Why do you ask?"

"Well, I could definitely use that kind of robot because my team, Organizational Development, has developed highly effective e-mail verbiage for all of our leaders and salespeople."

"What's the problem?" I asked, sensing a big opportunity.

Harold sighed.

"Our people lose the verbiage. And we lose sales when our leaders communicate the wrong ideas or information."

"Good news!" I cried.

I leaped onto my desk but got tangled in my cape and tripped, crashing to the floor. Luckily, the only thing that was bruised was my ego. I heard a muffled chuckle from my star pupil as I hopped back onto the desk.

"Good news!" I tried again. "Now, your people can *and will* use that important verbiage!"

"But how?" Harold asked, trying not to laugh at my klutziness.

"Harold the Hamster," I said, "meet your next robot, the Draftinator. It will help you rapidly insert drafts, templates, and snippets into e-mail and documents."

Harold looked around the room, half expecting a robot to emerge from my supply closet.

"The robot is *here*," I said, pointing to his computer. I hopped off my desk and hoisted Harold back onto my chair.

"Show me one of the snippets you just mentioned," I said encouragingly.

Harold opened a document titled, *Important Sales Verbiage*. I made a couple quick adjustments and then had Harold open a new e-mail.

"Now, click your mouse here, here, and here."

Harold clicked as instructed, and his eyes opened wide with amazement.

"Pow!" he cried. "The snippet's in the e-mail. I've been wasting so much time, cutting and pasting verbiage into e-mail messages. The Draftinator is going to save everyone time at Foster and Schrubb."

"Agreed," I said. "And I'll show you how to use the Draftinator in Word, Outlook, Lotus Notes, and Gmail.

That way you can spread the word to all the good people of Planet Earth."

Harold peered at me suspiciously.

"Planet Earth?"

"There is a bit more to this costume than meets the eye, Harold. I'll explain in a while, but first, it's time for you to activate the Draftinator with a few easy steps."

"Check!" Harold said, thumbing to the correct place in the *ZIP!* Tips book. "Let me try one now."

"How about trying five?" I asked.

"Why five?"

"Repetition is the mother of all knowledge," I said. "Here is the next core *ZIP!* Tips principle."

CORE PRINCIPLE #4

See One. Do Five. Teach Ten.

"That makes sense," Harold said. "You want me to watch one *ZIP!* Tip and then practice it five times to get the hang of it and then teach it to my team so everyone wins."

"You're a natural zipper." I laughed. "Now get cracking!"

ROBOT: THE DRAFTINATOR

JOB: Rapidly adds commonly used snippets and passages to save tons of time and improve communication quality.

The Draftinator for Outlook and Word 2007, 2010, and 2013 ("Quick Parts")

Note: Does not work in Outlook 2003 or Mac Outlook 2011.

- Highlight any frequently used text, graphic, or snippet within an Outlook e-mail or Word document.
- Click on *Insert* > *Quick Parts* > *Save Selection*.
- Name your selection and click on *OK*.
- To retrieve: Click where you want to place the Quick Part inside your e-mail or document.
- Click on *Insert* > *Quick Parts* and a drop-down menu will show all the Quick Parts you stored.
- Click on your item to instantly paste it into your e-mail or document.
- To delete or edit a Quick Part, click on *Insert* > *Quick Parts*, right-click on any item, and then select *Organize and Delete*.

The Draftinator for Gmail ("Canned Responses")

- From Gmail e-mail, click on the gear icon in the upper-right corner.
- Click on *Settings* > *Labs*.
- Select *Enable Canned Responses* and click on the *Save Changes* button at the bottom of the page.
- To create a canned response, open a new e-mail and enter your text, graphic, or snippet.

- Click on *Canned responses.*
- Click on *New canned response,* name the response, and then click on *OK.*
- To use your canned response, open a new e-mail, and then click on *Canned responses.*
- Select one of the templates you have stored.
- Edit and *Send.*

The Draftinator for Lotus Notes ("Stationary")

- From your inbox, click on *Tools > Stationary > New Stationary > Message.*
- Add your draft snippet and click on *Save.*
- Name your snippet and click on *OK.*
- To use, go to *Tools > Stationary* and double-click on your draft.

The Draftinator for Mac Word 2011 ("AutoText")

- Open a Mac Word document.
- Create and highlight your snippet.

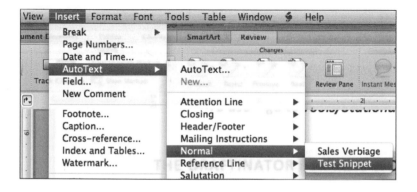

- On the topmost menu, click on *Insert* > *AutoText* > *New.*
- Name your snippet and click on *OK.*
- To use your snippet, go to the topmost menu and click on *Insert* > *AutoText* > *Normal.*
- Select your snippet.

THE TRANSFORMER

Instantly Morph E-mail into Other Useful Things

"So what did you mean about Planet Earth earlier?" Harold asked.

"Do you feel overloaded, overwhelmed, and over-worked?" I asked.

"Doesn't everyone?"

"Well, I was sent here from another planet to help defeat the dark forces of chaos and—"

"What in the world are these dark forces you keep babbling about?" Harold demanded.

"The Darkonians," I said.

"Who are they?"

"They're nasty, green aliens bent on taking over the universe by making helpless hamsters of you all. They've been blasting Planet Earth with a powerful weapon called the chaos beam for almost a hundred years. This weapon is what turned you into a hamster. I've been sent to help you fight back."

Harold clearly was not buying my story. He folded his arms in front of him.

"And where exactly are you from?"

"Why, Planet P, of course."

Harold shot me a sarcastic look. "So you're Z from Planet P?"

"That's right. *P* for productivity."

I had my fists on my hips again, giving Harold my best superhero profile pose.

A tiny snicker escaped from underneath Harold's little hamster whiskers.

"What's so funny?"

"Z from P!" Harold smirked. He tried to stop laughing, but that only made his guffaws stronger.

"You can laugh if you want, Harold, but the chaos of jammed inboxes, lost information, out-of-control meetings—it's only going to get worse unless you all fight back by using *ZIP!* Tips. In fact, here's the next core principle of *ZIP!*"

 **Core Principle #5**

Whoever Manages Their Chaos the Best Wins.

Harold calmed down a bit and nodded. "In a 24-7, always-connected world that's overloaded with information and interruptions, that makes a lot of sense. But let's stop with this alien nonsense and get back to the *ZIP!* Tips. I admit they're pretty useful, Z."

"The 'alien stuff' is—oh, never mind," I said. "I know you have less than three hours before your press conference."

Harold looked nervously at his watch.

"More like two and a half hours now."

"Okay, the next robot we're going to activate is the Transformer."

ROBOT: THE TRANSFORMER

JOB: Transforms ordinary e-mails into scheduled to-do items, appointments, meetings, contacts, and much more.

"Transformers?" Harold asked, looking puzzled. "Isn't that a movie featuring vehicles that morph into incredible spacebots?"

"Yes, the Transformers and I go way back." I sighed, reminiscing a moment. "But in today's *ZIP!* Tip revolution they can be powerful shape shifters. They can change an e-mail into a task or calendar item in the blink of an eye. They can also help you build a fantastic social media network."

Harold frowned. "Shape shifters?"

I slowly approached Harold's computer as if I were approaching a bomb that needed defusing.

"Buckle your seat belt, Harold, and stand back. This is pretty intense stuff!"

Harold jumped up in his chair, eagerly watching my every move.

- I slowly left-clicked on an e-mail, dragged it to the lower-left corner of his Outlook window, and hovered it precariously over Outlook's calendar icon.

"Are you ready?" I looked at Harold who was breathless with excitement.

When Harold nodded nervously, I let go of the e-mail and shouted: "Transform!"

A flash of light and a tremendous boom filled the room. Harold was thrust high into the air, and when he landed, he scurried under my meeting table. Startled, I looked out the window and realized a huge thunderstorm had rolled in. The Darkonians were turning up the power of the chaos beam. Apparently they didn't like the progress we were making.

Slowly, Harold crawled out from under the table and gasped. He eyed his computer with newfound awe. The e-mail had magically transformed into an Outlook calendar invitation!

"No way!" he cried. "This robot can't be that powerful!"

"But it is, Harold! Your e-mail is now a meeting. It's a great way to build a task into your e-calendar, so you won't forget to do it."

"Right!" Harold cried. "And if I get an e-mail relevant to a meeting, I can zip it into my calendar, and it'll get synched to my smartphone, or tablet. That . . . that eliminates so many steps!" Harold blurted, eyes glimmering.

"But wait!" I held up a finger, and used my best, late-night infomercial voice. "There's more."

- You can also drag an e-mail to the Tasks icon to instantly add it to your to-do list.

"Now, what would you pay? Oh, wait! These *ZIP!* Tips are free . . ."

"No way!" Harold said reverently, ignoring my feeble attempts at humor. "That was too easy!"

"You try it."

Harold leaped up into the chair and carefully left-clicked and dragged an e-mail over the *Tasks* icon, paused, and let it go.

"Bam!" I cried, and once again, a thunderbolt of lightning shot out of the sky and my office lights flickered. My startled student scurried back under the meeting table.

"Wow!" Harold whispered from his hiding place. His whiskered nose peeked out from under the table, just a little bit. "Does that lightning strike every time you transform something?"

"Not every time." I turned from the window, grinning mischievously. "It's just an angry reaction from the Darkonians. They don't like it when someone learns to *ZIP!* Now be a brave hamster and get back up here."

Harold timidly climbed back up on the chair.

"I'm still a Darkonian skeptic," Harold whispered, nervously glancing out the window, "but I'm becoming a big

ZIP! Tip fan. Okay, I know the drill. See one; do five, and—after my press conference—teach ten."

Harold tried another Transformer trick, and mercifully, the lightning held off this time. The corners of Harold's mouth twitched into a big toothy grin.

"So," Harold said when he was done performing five Transformer tasks, "what else can my Outlook Transformer do?"

- Lotus Notes, GroupWise, Entourage, and several other e-mail systems also allow you to do similar transformations. Outlook for Mac unfortunately doesn't, yet. So far, Gmail only lets you drag e-mails into folders, but I bet they're working on more Transformers too.

Since you use **Outlook for PC**, let's look at some very special features that you should try," I said, casting an anxious glance out the window.

"Such as?" Harold prompted.

- Right-click this time, while you drag an e-mail with an attachment into your calendar or Task folder.

Harold right-clicked and dragged an Outlook e-mail into his calendar, and this time when he let go, he gasped. The Transformer in Outlook popped up a small rectangular menu with some interesting options.

"Wow!" he cried. "My robot is asking me a question. I've got some great choices too."

"Exactly! So give it an order!" I encouraged him. "For example, select *Move* and the Transformer will move that

e-mail with the attachment into your calendar *and* delete it from your inbox in one click."

"I could use this when there's an attachment that I need for a task or meeting! Let me try this option," Harold cried, clicking on another option.

"Transform!" he yelled, and he grinned wildly as an e-mail with a spreadsheet zipped into his calendar as an attachment. Then he clicked on the attachment in his calendar event, and the e-mail opened with the spreadsheet inside it.

"Good robot! Nice little shape shifter," Harold said affectionately.

"All I ask," I said seriously, "is that you remember to delete the attachments from your calendar when the meeting is done. You don't want to slow down the e-mail system by saving too many big items in your calendar."

"Yes, sir!" Harold saluted. "Hey, didn't you say something about social media?"

I smiled. "I saved the most powerful Outlook Transformer for last."

Harold suddenly remembered something and frowned. "I don't know how much networking I can do in this state," he lamented, staring at his paws and furry little feet.

"In good time, Harold, all in good time."

- Now, click and drag an e-mail, but this time drop it onto your Outlook Contacts icon, the one you click on to open up your address book.

Harold dutifully did as he was told. "What?" he cried in shock. "The e-mail transforms into a new contact with the name and e-mail address prepopulated!"

"Which is a megarapid way to build more contacts, experts, clients, and friends into your Outlook address book."

- Click on *View > People Pane > Normal* to activate this robot.

Harold turned to me giddily. "This will help me build my network."

"Right." I nodded. "And a new feature of Outlook 2010 and 2013 is the *Social Media Connector.*

- Once you've added a contact to Outlook, click on the double arrow at the bottom-right corner of your screen.
- Then, click on the horizontal bar at the very bottom of the screen within that contact and drag it up to reveal the social media area. Click on the silhouetted image and the green plus sign

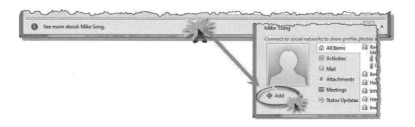

in order to add that person to your Linkedin, Facebook, Xing, My Site, or other social media network."

Harold looked shocked as he played with his new robot. "Wait a minute, this also sorts all the e-mail I've gotten from a particular contact, and I can sort by *All Items, Mail, Attachments, Meetings*, and more. Amazing!"

Harold thought for a second.

"So now I have an incredibly fast way to build my social network and a brand new way to search and sort within Outlook. And imagine how helpful this will be for our sales team members. They're going to become relationship-building experts!"

"Yes, indeed." I laughed, feeling a warm glow in my heart. My mission to change the world was off to a great start.

"Now, I'm going to transform five messages into contacts to burn this puppy into my brain," Harold said with gusto.

But each time he transformed something, he nervously looked out the window, expecting another tremendous boom of thunder and lightning.

"Something big is about to happen, Harold," I said, motioning toward the windows in my office. "But it won't be coming from *those* windows . . ."

THE ZIP ZONE

Fast Access to Everything That Matters Most

As we stared out of the windows of my high-rise office, the bustling city below seemed even more frenetic than usual. Pedestrians were scurrying around in a sudden downpour, trying to find cover.

Harold and I squinted down at the crowd.

"I'm seeing more and more hamsters down there," Harold noticed. I could tell he was beginning to wonder if the Darkonians were real after all.

"I've surveyed more than 50,000 professionals," I said. "Guess the percentage of professionals who say they need a better way to find their info fast?"

"50 percent?"

"No, 93 percent![3] Everyone is spending a huge amount of time searching and clicking to locate the right document at the right time."

---

3. Mike Song, "The Tech Opportunity: How Everyday Tech Skills Can Boost Performance, Productivity, and Profits," GetControl.net/blog, 2013.

"Click, click, click." Harold sighed with an air of futility. "We're clicking our lives away."

I pointed at a blue coffee-shop awning ten stories down. "Hey, don't you wish you could click on that Blue Sky Café sign and instantly have a chocolaty, rich mochaccino in your hand?"

Harold closed his eyes and sniffed, as if the aroma of coffee were in the air. "Yes . . ." he sighed. Then his eyes popped open. "Don't tell me there's a robot for that!" he exclaimed hopefully.

"No." I laughed. "Don't I wish! We'll head down there in a bit, but my point is that feeling of clicking and getting exactly what you want is visceral, isn't it? It's kind of a universal human fantasy."

"It's a hamster fantasy too," Harold said wistfully. "But yes, you're right. We're an instant-gratification nation."

He pretended to tap on the Blue Sky Café sign from ten stories up and then sighed. "But it's impossible, Z."

I shook my head. "Not when it comes to the work world, the Windows world. In that virtual world you can click things and bam!" I snapped my fingers in front of Harold's twitching, bewhiskered nose. "In a nanosecond you've got exactly what you want. All you need to do is activate the Zip Zone robot."

"Zip Zone?" Harold grinned. "Uh, that sounds kind of personal, Z."

"No, it's not!" I said, leading Harold back to the desk. "There are almost a billion Windows users on this planet,

Harold. And 99 percent[4] of them have never activated this robot."

"Show me the way," Harold said, turning his laptop toward me. I clicked on his lower-right Windows toolbar.

"How cruel. Your Zip Zone robot—this area here—is locked up like a prisoner," I pointed out.

"That violates an important core *ZIP!* principle."

CORE PRINCIPLE #6

Create One-Click Access to What Matters Most.

In a flash, I reconfigured Harold's lower toolbar and asked him to point out important, frequently used items. He gasped as I showed him that he now had one-click access to a wide variety of useful applications and documents.

"Now I have all my most useful shortcuts on my lower-right, horizontal toolbar," Harold mused. "The Zip Zone is incredibly useful because it's the *one thing* in Windows that's almost always visible. I can see my Zip Zone when

---

4. Ibid.

I'm in working in Outlook, surfing the web, or editing a Word document."

Example of Activated Zip Zone Robot

"Your Zip Zone robot is an easy-to-use power portal," I said reverently, "a wormhole to what matters most. And like you said, it's open 24-7."

Harold was getting excited. "So the Zip Zone robot works for Outlook e-mail and documents? And other stuff too?"

"Yes."

"Important document folders?"

"Yes."

"Shared drive and SharePoint folders?"

"Yes."

"Websites I visit all the time?"

"Yes. You simply click and drag the small icon to the left of the browser web address down to your Zip Zone.."

"Applications?"

"Sure. Try any highly trafficked item that has an icon. And you can delete them anytime without destroying anything, because once something is placed in your Zip Zone, it becomes a Windows shortcut. Just right-click and select *Delete*."

"Brilliant," Harold mused with a grin.

I deactivated Harold's Zip Zone so he could get the feel of setting it up on his own.

"Harold, here are the instructions to activate your Zip Zone robot for Windows XP, 7, and 8. I also have instructions for Mac users."

"Good." Harold nodded. "I've got friends using all different operating systems."

It only took Harold sixty seconds to reactivate his Zip Zone robot. He spent a few minutes zooming in and out of his most-used items.

"This is so much faster!" he cried. "It's like I've been crawling to my documents in slow motion with a cement block tied to my back."

"You're sipping at light speed now," I replied.

Again, I felt that rush of excitement and energy that comes with helping someone *ZIP!* I closed my eyes and heard my mom's voice. "Don't just sit on the couch, watching TV," she would say. "Get up and make yourself useful!"

How am I doing, Mom?

ROBOT: THE ZIP ZONE

JOB: Creates rapid, always-available access to your most important and frequently used documents, folders, applications, and websites.

Zip Zone for XP, Windows 7 and 8

Note: These instructions assume that your Windows toolbar is positioned at the bottom of your monitor's screen. Windows 8 users should open a Word document at this time.

- Right-click on your lower, horizontal toolbar, just right of center.
- Uncheck *Lock the Taskbar* if it is checked.
- Right-click again and click on *Toolbars* and check *Links*.
- A dotted bar will appear with the word *Links* next to it in the lower-right corner. Pull the *Links* bar to the left to create more space for your Zip Zone robot.
- You will see a problem. Only a couple icons will fit in the Zip Zone area because the text in their titles takes up too much space. To correct this problem, right-click on the word *Links* and uncheck the words *Show Text*.
- Now you can create shortcuts for what matters most. Drag and drop documents, folders, shared drive folders, SharePoint folders, applications, and shortcuts to websites to the Zip Zone to create one-click access to your most important stuff.
- **Bonus *ZIP!* Tip:** You can add colorful icons to change generic-looking Zip Zone items to speed navigation. You will notice that an Excel spreadsheet shows up as a generic Excel icon. To make it visually clear, right-click on the icon and select *Properties* > *Shortcut* and *Change Icon*. This will usually lead you to a bunch of icons. Select one that has meaning for you and click on *Apply* and *OK*. The appearance of your Zip Zone icon will change immediately. If for some reason you don't see any icons, there are many websites that offer free icons.

Zip Zone for Mac Users

Note: These instructions were created for Mac Mountain Lion OS. You can place websites, documents, and folders on the right side of your lower, horizontal dock area.

- **Documents and Folders:** Determine your most-used documents and folders and drag them to your rightmost, bottom dock area. In some cases, you may be able to drag Share Drive Folders or SharePoint folders.
- I recommend changing the icons of folders and documents to distinguish them. There are many websites that offer free icons.
  - To change the icons on your folders, press the Control key and click on the folder.
  - Click on *Get Info*.
  - Click and drag the icon graphic into the smaller folder at the top right of the *Get Info* window. If this does not change the icon, you should be able to open the graphic, select *All* via the Command + A key, copy using the Command + C key, and paste the icon into the *Get Info* folder using Control + V.
- **Websites:** Choose three or four of your most-used websites and drag them to the same dock area on the lower right. Click and drag the icon to the left of any URL and the website will move down the lower-right toolbar.

"This is amazing!" Harold said with a big grin. Then he glanced at the clock on my wall, and his smile faded.

"I'm running out of time. What's next, Z?"

I pointed out the window where a powerful storm continued to rage.

"To the Blue Sky Café to discover smartphone and tablet *ZIP!* Tips. Don't worry, Harold. We'll get you to the press conference on time."

THE AUTODIALER

6

Dial Teleconference Numbers and Pass Codes with One Tap

As the elevator to the lobby descended, I turned to Harold.

"The world is changing, and so are you. You're starting to look a bit more human, my friend."

"Huh?" Harold said hopefully. He glanced at his reflection in the mirrored elevator wall and smiled. The *ZIP!* Tips were beginning to take hold.

Gasps, whispers, and giggles could be heard as we rushed down the street and into the coffee shop, soaking wet from the rain. We made our way to the counter and ordered two mochaccinos.

"Hey, Aquaman, you might want to try a few sit-ups!" one of the customers joked.

"I'm working on it!" I smiled, making a mental note to hit the gym right after my talk with my tailor.

I was surprised to see that almost half of the patrons were hamsters. We found a table and I took a long, satisfying sip of my chocolaty drink. Mmmmm.

The storm was raging outside, and the moment had come to expand the movement against the Darkonians and their dastardly deeds. I gathered my strength to stand and address the coffee-shop patrons.

"Hamsters, humans, and countrypersons," I boomed in my best stage voice, "bring forth your devices! Your smartphones, tablets, laptops, anything mobile upon which you work. The *ZIP!* era has arrived, and the time has come to unleash the power of your robots so you can achieve the success you deserve."

The crowd fell into an awkward who-is-this-nut? silence. Patrons glanced nervously at each other.

Harold timidly spoke up. "Everyone listen, this is Z, and . . . I know he looks goofy, and he thinks he's from outer space, but he can teach you a new way to work. He's a productivity superhero. So take out your phones, tablets, and laptops and learn a few *ZIP!* Tips."

A young hamster piped in. "What's a *ZIP!* Tip?"

"A quick and easy tech tip. Time management is out and tech management is in," Harold said excitedly, pointing his half-human, half-hamster paw at me. "He'll show you!"

A few crowd members left, scoffing, but most stayed and rummaged through their pockets and bags for their devices.

"Let's get started!" I cried. A sea of laptops, smart-phones, and tablets appeared, held up by hands and hamster paws alike.

"Bring it, Flash!" encouraged a portly female hamster in front.

"Um, it's Z, but . . . okay, I'm 'bringin' it," I said with a smile.

"Here are a few, quick writing tips. First, stop typing apostrophes on your smartphone or tablet. Open an e-mail and type the words *cant*, *dont*, and *wont* without the apostrophes."

"Hey!" a hip young hamster piped. "AutoCorrect fills them in."

"Right!" Harold exclaimed, Robin to my Batman. "See, your phone is a robot. Make *it* do the work."

This time, I heard whispers of approval, and I saw heads nodding.

"Now, everyone, type this sentence into your device: 'I will get more done.' But instead of typing a period at the end, tap the space bar twice and start typing another sentence."

"Nice!" the well dressed lady hamster shouted, turning to a colleague. "It added a period and a space and capitalized the first letter of the next sentence."

"A three-for-one bargain!" Harold yelped.

"Now, raise your hand, or paw, if you have a teleconference or voice-mail phone number that you call a few times a day."

Just about all of them raised their hand.

"Usually, you have to dial the first number, wait for the phone to ring, and then type in one or two more codes when prompted."

"I hate that!" someone yelled.

Why not train your robot to dial both numbers for you so that you can focus on other things?"

"How?" "Show us!" the crowd cried.

"Most smartphone users can simply add three commas or three letter *p*'s after the main telephone number within Outlook, Lotus, or Gmail and then synchronize their address book with their phone. Each comma or *p* instructs the phone to wait for two seconds so that it dials the second number after the call is answered."

"I want to try it now," a sharply dressed businesswoman exclaimed.

"Okay," I said, "let's do it right here, right now."

ROBOT: THE AUTODIALER

JOB: Saves thousands of taps per year by having the phone dial secondary phone numbers.

The AutoDialer for iPhone

- Open the address book contact for your teleconference or voice-mail.
- Select *Edit.*
- Then tap to the right of the first phone number and select +*#.
- Tap *Pause.*
- Do this two more times so that you have three commas after the number.
- Enter the pass-code number after the commas.
- Tap *Done.*

The AutoDialer for Android Phones

Note: Some android phones may have different instructions.

- Open the address book contact for your teleconference number.
- Select *Menu* and *Edit.*
- Tap to the right of the first phone number and select *P* for *Pause* three times.
- You will see three commas appear behind the phone number.
- Type the pass-code number after the commas.
- Tap *Save.*

The AutoDialer for BlackBerry Phones

- Open the address book contact for your teleconference number.
- Tap the menu button, which is the one with seven dots on it, to the left of your track pad.
- Tap *Edit.*
- Tap to the right of the first phone number.
- Tap the menu button again and select *Add Pause* three times.
- You will see three *p*'s behind the phone number.
- Type the pass code after the *p*'s.
- Tap your back button, which is to the right of the track pad, and then select *Save.*

Harold and the crowd quickly made the setting changes and looked to me for the next step.

"Now listen up, everyone," I said. "Put your phones on speaker and dial that teleconference number. Then hold up your phones."

The crowd dialed and raised their phones high, and suddenly the room was filled with phone beeps as the dial tones from the first numbers were speed dialed.

Then there was a brief six-second pause, and suddenly the room was filled with noises as sixty telephonic robots autodialed a second pass code. The crowd erupted in cheers, realizing that they'd just eliminated a ton of keystrokes.

I noticed that some were Tweeting the *ZIP!* Tips to friends, using the hashtag, #ziptip.

The Tower of Learning Power

Optimize Your Smartphone and Tablet Home Page

Harold, sensing I was about to deliver a coup de grâce, rang out, "But wait! There's more!"

"Yes, my friend, there *is* more," I said, turning back to the café crowd. "How many people here want a fantastic performance review? How many of you would like to be recognized as the best in your field? How many of you would like to be the top-selling salesperson or top leader at your organization?"

Hands and paws shot up around the room.

"And how many of you want to fritter away your life playing idle games and achieving mediocrity?"

One guilty-looking hamster raised his hand at the back of the room. Realizing he was alone in his complete lack of ambition, he backed up toward the door and ran smack into the knees of a cameraman from a local television crew. They had been alerted by the Tweets, Facebook postings, and YouTube videos that my small but growing audience was posting. Apparently, my little impromptu public address was becoming a newsworthy event.

I cleared my throat and continued my message as the camera's red recording light beamed in my direction.

"Friends, our work devices have become instant gratification, nonstop notification, endless procrastination, temptation stations."

The crowd was silent, and Harold shot me a worried look. Then, a techy-looking guy, in front, stood up.

"I think I see what you're getting at," he said. "Every morning, my home page leads me *away* from achieving my goals. I get up and there are my games, tunes, and news feeds. I could spend an hour on Facebook or Twitter just chatting or gaming the morning away."

The crowd murmured in agreement. "The fun stuff can be distracting." "I can't stop checking Facebook." "I feel the urge to IM someone every nine seconds." "Help! I can't stop playing *Rabid Zombie Rabbits.*"

"The secret is to change your device's home page into a *success and learning center,*" I explained. "In five minutes you can shift it from performance drainer to productivity gainer."

"How?" someone yelled.

I held up a woman's android and said, "Let me show you how to turn your home page into a **Tower of Learning Power** robot! Quick! To your home page. Let's begin!"

ROBOT: THE AMAZING TOWER OF LEARNING POWER

JOB: Organizes and prioritizes your home page to maximize performance.

Step 1: Zap Your Time-Wasting Apps

"First, I want you to move all of your tempting, time-wasting apps off your home page. You don't have to get rid of them; just get them off your home page. They're not your first priority. Then, we'll replace them with apps and info that help you achieve more every day."

"But how?" a confused bystander asked.

"On most tablets and phones, like androids, iPhones, and iPads, you simply press and hold any icon, and it can be dragged to another page. Move them at least two screens away from your home page. Sometimes the icon will slip off your finger, but believe in the power of *ZIP!* and try pressing and holding just a little bit harder."

The crowd dutifully began to move their time wasters off the home page. I saw a lot of smiles as they realized that they could get control of this area.

"I also recommend setting up some boundaries for habit-forming apps like Facebook. If you find you're wasting time, try the **Facebook 5 x 5** strategy. Look at Facebook for five minutes a day after 5 PM. You can also turn off notifications that tend to pull you away from being productive."

The crowd made some setting changes, and one man even created a folder called "5 x 5 Time Wasters." This put those tempting apps just a little farther away.

Step 2: Create Career Success Folders on the Second Row from the Top

"Okay, now that all those time wasters are gone, it's time to power up your home page by creating useful business folders. For example, why not create a folder with all your most useful business apps inside? I have a folder packed with tools to make my smartphone and tablet keynote talks more exciting and useful. You could also create folders for business travel, file sharing, or document-management apps. The big idea is to assemble and organize the tools that bring you productivity and success right on your home page."

Again, I heard some murmurs of confusion, and one hamster squeaked, "How do you create folders? We all use different devices."

I felt an odd buzzing in my right arm, and suddenly it involuntarily shot up, spinning me around to point at the wall above the cash register. Out of my finger emanated a quick flash of light, and suddenly three Power-Point-looking instruction slides appeared. There was one for iPhone/iPads, androids, and BlackBerry smartphones.

Gasps emanated from the crowd, but no one was more surprised than I was. It seemed that my powers were growing as I shared ideas with an ever-widening number of people.

"It's easy," I cried, leaping up onto the coffee bar. "Follow these instructions."

"I'm getting organized!" Harold shouted as he created his first smart folder and moved it to the second row from the top of his iPad home page.

"Easy access to my most useful apps!" a reporter shouted. "Do you mind if I post these to Twitter?"

"Not at all," I said, noticing that a lot of people were filming each step. "Spread the word as far and wide as you can!"

Create a Success Folder on an iPhone or iPad

Note: Primary Apple apps, such as mail or settings, can't be placed in folders, but anything else can.

- Press and hold any icon until all icons begin to vibrate.
- Drag and drop one icon into another to create a folder.
- Name the folder anything you like.
- You can drag more icons into your folder.
- Tap the *Home* button to stop the vibration.

Create a Success Folder on Most Android Devices

Note: Folder creation on the android operating system may differ for different phone and manufacturers.

- Press and hold any empty part of your screen, and you will see a *Personalize* area where you can select *Folder* and then *New Folder.*
- A new folder will pop to your screen.
- Open it up and press and hold the current title in the top-left area. It's preset to the word *Folder.*

- A *Rename* box pops up, allowing you to title it whatever you want.
- Drag and drop icons into your new folder.

Create a Success Folder on a Blackberry

- Tap the BlackBerry menu button, which is the one with seven dots on it, to the left of the track pad, and then select *Add Folder.*
- Name the folder (for example, "Travel") and tap *Add.*
- Now, tap any application (e.g., United Airlines Travel app) that you'd like to move and select *Move to Folder.*
- You will see all a list of all folders. Tap the one you created to add your app.

Step 3: Create a Top Row of High-Power Learning Icons

When the buzz settled down and everyone had their second row of Success Folders set up, I turned to a smart-looking female hamster and asked, "What's the name of a high-level thought leader who has taught you a great deal via the web?"

"Well, I'm in social media marketing, and I've learned a ton from Seth Godin and Paul Gillin," she said, peering over her really cool-looking glasses.

"If Seth and Paul came to your office and taught you something every day, would it help you succeed?"

"Of course! They're brilliant!"

"I want you all to think about four people who could help you get better at your job. Who are the thought leaders in your world?"

The room exploded as people exchanged the names of all the brilliant men and women they admired. I let them mingle ideas and then put my fingers to my lips, and the room quieted. The TV reporter nudged her cameraman and whispered, "Zoom in for this bit here . . ."

I whispered for effect, "If you love these people so much, why don't you invite them into your office every day?"

Harold looked nervous. "But how? That would cost a fortune!"

"I mean your virtual office, your device's home page. You can pop a link to any web page you want on to your home page, and every time you've got a moment to learn, you tap the icon and kapow! You're getting great advice from the experts you respect."

"Or I could play my tenth game of *Rabid Zombie Rabbits*!" Harold joked. Everyone laughed.

"A Tower of *Learning* Power!" the female exec cried. "I get it. We ditch the fluffy apps, create a row of powerful business folders, and then develop a top row of icons for people we consider to be . . . well, icons in their fields."

I nodded. "I'd also recommend creating a link to your organization's training website. These days, you might be able to actually take an e-course on your device."

"Smart!" the female exec said.

"The Tower of Learning Power leads us to the next core *ZIP!* Tip principle," I said.

CORE PRINCIPLE #7

Optimize Your Home Page for Career Success.

"Okay, I just need to share a few more things," I said.

As the TV producer and cameraman busily recorded my every extraterrestrial move, I proceeded to help all of them build their Towers of Learning Power. I would later learn that more than a billion e-mails, Tweets, and Facebook posts exploded at that moment around the entire world as *ZIP! Tips* went viral.

"Now, listen up, everybody," I said. "I want to show you how to create shortcuts to Tower of Learning Power websites. So, open your primary browser and surf to a website or blog you find extremely useful."

Here are the instructions I shared with the café crowd.

Shortcuts to Tower of Learning Power Websites for iPhone and iPad

- Open your Safari browser and surf to a website or blog that will provide you with extremely useful knowledge.
- Find the rectangular box with an arrow jumping out of it. The box is in the upper-left of an iPad, and on an iPhone, it is on the bottom, in the center.
- Tap the box that has an arrow jumping out of it and select *Add to Homescreen*.
- Rename the web page with a shorter name of seven letters or less.

- Tap *Add*.
- Find the icon (it isn't always on your home screen) and press and hold it so you can move it to the top row of your home screen. Repeat until the top row is filled with experts.

Shortcuts to Tower of Learning Power Websites for Androids

Note: Some androids may work slightly differently since they are made by different companies.

- Open your android browser and surf to a website or blog that will provide you with extremely useful knowledge.
- Tap the menu button and select *Add bookmark*.
- Rename the bookmark with a shorter name of seven letters or less.
- Press and hold an empty space on your home screen until the *Personalize* menu appears.
- Select *Shortcut* and then *Bookmark*.
- Select the Tower of Learning Power bookmark you created from the bookmarks page that appears.

Shortcuts to Tower of Learning Power Websites for Blackberry Smartphones

- Open your BlackBerry browser and surf to a website or blog that will provide you with extremely useful knowledge.

- Tap the BlackBerry menu button, which is the one with seven dots on it, usually found to the left of your track pad.
- Select *Add to Homescreen.*
- Rename the web page with a shorter name of seven letters or less.
- Make sure *Home* is the selected location and that *Favorite* is checked
- Tap *Add.*
- Find the icon by tapping *All* on your main screen and then highlight the icon with your track pad. Tap the menu button and tap *Move.* This allows you to use the track pad to move the icon to the top row of the BlackBerry home page.

Important Note: The Tower of Learning Power can be implemented in many places including Windows XP, 7, and 8 home screens. The Windows 8 start page is also an ideal location for the Tower of Learning Power robot.

THE SEARCHBOT

New Ways to Zing with Google and Bing

The café crowd buzzed with anticipation as they built their Towers of Learning Power. I glanced down at Harold and saw that he had begun to look even more human. Other hamsters in the room also seemed more relaxed and less jumpy.

Harold glanced at his watch and shot me a panicked look. "I've got less than an hour, Z!"

I nodded and decided to launch a rapid-fire barrage of *ZIP!* Tips to help Harold and the crowd.

"Listen up! *Search* is a robot too! There are almost 1.5 billion people who use Google or Bing to search for info," I cried. "Here are ten ways you can activate your **Searchbots!**"

ROBOT: THE SEARCHBOT

JOB: Zips to helpful information in search engines.

"Zip away!" a CEO near the door cried, holding his tablet up, ready to snap a picture.

"From almost any search engine on any device . . ." I began, and with rapid fire, I shot each of these *ZIP!* Tips from my new superhero finger onto a new spot on the wall. The crowd spun in place, trying each *ZIP!* Tip as it appeared, and some were even snapping a picture of the instructions and sending them to friends and colleagues.

1. **The Weather Fetcher:** Get a fast weather forecast by typing in your postal code plus the word *temp.*

"Oooh," the crowd murmured.

"This also works for movies," I added. "Type your postal code plus the word *movies.*"

2. **The Overnight Package Tracker:** Find any FedEx, UPS, or DHL package in a flash by simply typing the tracking number into your search engine. The carrier will give you a link without having to log into the carrier's website.

"Ziparoo!" a man cried in the back.

3. **The Flight Tracker:** Type in your airline and flight number to get an up-to-the-second report on arrival time, gate number, or delays—for example, type "United 235."

"What?" "No way!"

4. **The Converter:** This Searchbot converts almost anything in a flash: dollars to pesos, gallons to liters. Just

type the word *into* between whatever you want to convert—for example, "798 Euros into Yen."

"The Converter works for distance and temperature conversions too!" the hip-looking hamster cried.

5. **The Site Searcher:** Search for info on only one website by typing the word *site* followed by a colon, no space, and then the site name and a search term. For example, to sign up for *ZIP!* Tips classes, type: "site:zip-tips.com zip class." *Important: Do not put a space between the colon and the site name.*

"A shameless plug!" Harold cried.
"But useful!" The hipster hamster in black laughed.
"More!"

6. **The Specifier:** Placing quotes around any phrase or name gives search results for that precise term. This dramatically narrows your results to the exact thing you need—for example, search for "customized title widths version explorer" and you will get 34 million results. Next, search " 'customized title widths' version explorer" and you will get around seventy results.

"ZZZZZZZZ," the crowd buzzed happily.

"You can also use the quotes in other searches," I explained. "For example, in Outlook, type the phrase "out of office" in quotes, and you can find just the e-mails that contain that phrase in that exact order."

"Woo hoo!" someone in the crowd yelled.

7. **The Simplifier:** No need to capitalize, punctuate, use symbols, or even spell search terms perfectly. Google, Bing, and other search engines overlook all that stuff.

Harold slapped his head. "I've been punctuating everything for years. What a waste!"

"More! More!" the crowd shouted. To the delight of the audience, I shot my last few search-engine *ZIP!* Tips onto the wall. The audience swirled around to record them all. There were now four camera crews and about fifteen people filming on their phones.

8. **The Calculator:** Type any math equation into the search box and the answer will pop right out in an instant, along with a nice advanced-function calculator. Never fumble for a calculator again.

9. **The Dictionary:** Simply type the word *define* and any phrase or word for which you need a description, and your Searchbot delivers the dictionary definition in a flash.

Even the reporters were smiling as they tried every *ZIP!* on their tablets and phones.

10. **The Clock:** Simply type the word *time* and any city in the world to get the current time. This is a big help when scheduling meetings with a global group.

The café rippled with excited discussion as a chain reaction ripped through the crowd. They all seemed to be sharing their own incredible search-engine *ZIP!* Tips with each other.

THE VOLUME CRUSHER

Cuts Incoming E-mail by 20 to 40 Percent

As the crowd began to settle down after capturing my flurry of search-engine *ZIP!* Tips, a frustrated hamster in the back of the room timidly raised his hand.

"I appreciate all of this great advice, but I'm afraid."

"Of what?" I asked.

"The **Inbox Overload Monster**," he said in a shaky voice. A murmur ran through the crowd.

Someone hissed, "Don't say its name out loud!"

"Yeah, that only brings more e-mail," whispered a terrified hamster by the door.

"When we all get back to our offices, it will be there, waiting to cut us down," the hamster, on the verge of tears, continued. "Our inboxes will be jammed with thirty new e-mails, important requests, sometimes silly tasks, spam, and low-priority crap. Excuse my language . . ."

I nodded and said, "E-mail overload blows up deadlines, leads to miscommunication, and damages careers. It even locks people up in e-mail jail, forcing some organizations to shut down their e-mail system until they clean up the messages with big attachments.

"I'm in e-mail jail right now!" a man wailed in the back, holding up his laptop.

"I can help!" I cried, levitating temporarily to regain their focus. "It's time to activate the **Volume Crusher** robot for Outlook, Gmail, and Lotus Notes users."

"How does it work?" the teenage hamster barista behind the coffee bar asked.

"It filters all the *low-priority* e-mail from your inbox instantly."

The crowd gave a hopeful gasp.

"Where does it go?" someone asked.

"Low-priority e-mail will skip your inbox and go directly to folders that you check once or twice a month."

"The Volume Crusher moves them for us?"

"Yes. And if you do this for just a few weeks, you'll see a reduction in inbox clutter of 20 to 40 percent. "

"Show us!" the crowd cried. "Please!" "Now!"

I leaped to the frantic young man who had held up his PC, and I pressed a Wi-Fi button on my superhero utility belt. In a flash I had connected his laptop to the large HDTV screen over the counter so that all could see. Then I demonstrated how to activate the Volume Crusher robot.

Here are the instructions that I shared with the excited patrons of the Blue Sky Café.

ROBOT: THE VOLUME CRUSHER

JOB: Conquers e-mail overload by reducing inbox clutter.

The Volume Crusher for Outlook 2003 and 2007

- From the Outlook inbox, right-click on an e-mail.
- Select *Create Rule.*
- Check the top and bottom boxes on the left.
- Check *Select Folder* and click on the destination folder.
- Click on *New* to create a new folder if needed.

The Volume Crusher for Outlook 2010 and 2013

- From the Outlook Inbox, highlight any low-priority e-mail.
- Select *Rules > Always move messages from.*
- Click on the folder to which you want the e-mail to go.
- Click on *New* to create a new folder if needed.

The Volume Crusher for Gmail

- Check the box to the left of any Gmail e-mail.
- Click on *More > Filter messages like these.*
- Click on *Create filter with this search.*
- Check *Skip the Inbox* and *Apply the label > Choose Label.*
- Select *Label.*
- Click on *Create filter.*

The Volume Crusher for Lotus Notes

- Highlight any low-priority e-mail.
- Click on *More > Create Quickrule.*
- Check *When Sender* and *Select.*
- Choose or create folder.

THE ZIPCUT LIST

The Top-Ten Most Powerful Computer Shortcuts

A quick glance at Harold told me that the rapid *ZIP!* approach was working. I knew we were close to pulling him back into humanity. I decided to pull out all the stops.

"I'm going to count down the top-ten, most-useful, computer keyboard shortcuts of all time. I'll give you Windows first and then Mac. Discovering even one more shortcut can save you time every day!"

"Let's go!" the cameraman, who had put down his camera and pulled out his laptop, cried.

"Okay," I yelled.

"Coming in at number ten is the amazing Control + Z, or Command (⌘) + Z for Mac. This is a shortcut for *Undo*, but every time you strike the Z, it undoes another step."

"It's like a turbo reverse!" Harold shouted, rapidly undoing four steps with four clicks on the Z key while holding down his Control button. "This is going to make editing so much easier!"

"Figures you'd start with a Z tip!" a man in the back added. "That's right," I said, laughing and pointing at the letter Z on my chest. "I love the Z!"

I proceeded to countdown the shortcuts that would help all of them zip through their work.

ROBOT: THE ZIPCUTS

JOB: Help you work faster by reducing clicks and mental effort required to do your job.

Top-Ten Windows Computer Shortcuts

10. **Control + Z:** Undo multiple steps fast by hitting Z over and over again.

9. **Alt + Tab:** Toggle rapidly between all open programs.

8. **Windows Key + Tab:** Toggle through 3D view of open programs in Windows 7 and 8.

7. **Control + A:** Select all.

6. **Control + C:** Copy anything that is highlighted.

5. **Control + X:** Cut (and later copy) anything that is highlighted.

4. **Control + V:** Rapidly paste anything that has been copied.

3. **Control + F:** Instant keyword search of any document, e-mail, or web page.

2. **Control + the plus or minus sign:** Enlarge or decrease the viewing size of any web page.

1. **F12:** *File* > *Save As* for all Microsoft PC Office Documents: Save Outlook e-mail to your hard drive.

Top-Ten Mac Computer Shortcuts

10. **Command (⌘) + Z:** Undo multiple steps fast by hitting Z over and over again.
 9. **Command (⌘) + Tab:** Toggle rapidly between all open programs.
 8. **Command (⌘) + Shift + 3:** Take a screenshot.
 7. **Command (⌘) + A:** Select all.
 6. **Command (⌘) + C:** Copy anything that is high-lighted.
 5. **Command (⌘) + X:** Cut and later copy anything that is highlighted.
 4. **Command (⌘) | V:** Paste anything that has been copied.
 3. **Command (⌘) + F:** Instant keyword search of any document, e-mail, or web page.
 2. **Control + the plus or minus sign:** Enlarge or de-crease the viewing size of any web page.
 1. **Command (⌘) + Spacebar:** Open Spotlight Search.

The crowd cheered wildly as they practiced each tip. I knew our work was done at the café. I looked up at the bank of TV screens around the room and saw that the raucous *ZIP!* Tip session at the café was being beamed around the world on CNN, Fox, NBC, and other news outlets.

Outside in the rain, hundreds of hamsters, reporters, and business people were pressing up against the large glass windows. I knew it was time to get Harold out of there.

Quickly thanking the crowd—many of whom were looking a lot more human—for their attention, we dashed out of a back door, jumped into a taxicab, and were off to the press conference.

Harold turned to me and said, "I'm sorry I doubted you, Z. You really are from Planet P and here to save the world."

"I am," I replied, "but right now the only thing that matters is helping you save that press conference. Take out your laptop. I've got one more thing to show you."

THE COLLABORATOR

The Most Useful and Least Known Meeting Tool

The taxi sped off into the stormy afternoon, rounded a corner, and ran smack into a terrible traffic jam. Harold looked up from his computer.

"No. Not this. Not now!" he cried.

"Relax, Harold," I said. "It's just those evil green Darkonians and their chaos beam."

"They cause traffic jams?" Harold asked.

"And printer jams, computer-screen freezes, lost e-mails, meetings that go off course, and—"

"Are they the ones who make you lose your TV remote and car keys?" Harold interrupted.

"They sure are," I said grimly. "And they invented 'Reply to All'! It's only going to get worse unless everyone fights back with *ZIP!* Tips. But don't worry about the traffic jam. Leave the Darkonians to me. Right now, get online with your team via Microsoft OneNote."

"I don't have OneNote on my computer," Harold protested.

"Anyone with Microsoft Office for PC version 2010 or 2013 will have it. Many with Outlook 2007 have it too. It's an amazing productivity robot that almost no one has activated. Open your Microsoft Office folder under Programs and see if it's there. It's a purple icon with an *N* on it."

Harold clicked and opened OneNote for the first time. "Hmmm, what is this thing?"

"OneNote is a virtual workspace in the form of a flexible, digital notebook that can be accessed on a computer, tablet, or smartphone by members of your press conference team."

"Really?" Harold asked, peering at his screen.

"It's similar to another great **Collaborator** app called Evernote," I continued, "but I like OneNote because it integrates into other Microsoft Office programs like Outlook. For example, if you create a task in OneNote, the task is also created in your Outlook task list. OneNote allows you to create, share, and edit documents, notes, tasks, graphics, videos, and more with your team in a kind of powerful virtual binder."

"Perfect!" Harold said. "So I can use this for meetings notes, project management, and other team related activities!"

"And you can download free OneNote apps for your smartphone or tablet." I added.

I quickly showed Harold how to use OneNote and let him know that when he had more time he could take a twenty-minute class at Zip-Tips.com to gain even more experience.

ROBOT: THE COLLABORATOR

JOB: Provides a much better way to record meetings and projects in an easily shared digital format.

Create Your First OneNote Workbook and Begin Collaborating at the Next Level

Locate the OneNote icon by clicking on Windows *Start* > *All Programs* > *Microsoft Office* > *OneNote*.

Note: While OneNote is not yet available for Mac users, Evernote is a terrific and similar app that has many of the same features as OneNote.

- Once OneNote is open, click on *File* > *New* > *Web*.
- *You may need to log into or create a Microsoft Live ID or Skydrive account.*
- Name your folder.
- Select *Create Folder,* which is an icon that appears in the lower-right portion of your computer screen.
- OneNote will then prompt you to share this folder with others by e-mailing them a link.

Microsoft OneNote

Notebook created. It is accessible to anyone with permissions at that Web location. Do you want to e-mail someone about the notebook?

E-mail a Link   No, Thanks

Quick Start Instructions for OneNote

Creating Tabs

You can divide any notebook into useful sections by adding tabs across the top.

- Click the tab asterisk (2007, 2010) or tab plus sign (2013) at the top of any page to add and name a new section.
- Right-click on any tab to quickly rename, delete, or copy it. You can also right-click to change tab color or password-protect the section.

Creating Pages

Now you're almost ready to start taking notes. But first, notice that each tab area can be divided into sub-sections or pages that appear on the right. If you're taking meeting notes you may want to create a sub-page for action items and another sub-page for decisions that have been made by the team.

- You create a page by clicking *New Page.*
- You can name the new page by filling in the topic area in the blank space in the upper-left portion of each page.
- Right-click on any page to quickly rename, delete, or copy it. You can also right-click to change tab color or password-protect the section.

Click anywhere to begin adding meeting notes.

- Click the *Insert* button to add a wide variety of content.
- Click the green *Synchronize* button so your changes will be updated for your entire team.
- To learn more, consider taking the Get Control! One-Note class at Zip-Tips.com.

The taxi was stuck in a traffic jam, but Harold was not. I watched in amazement as he began to collaborate with his team via OneNote. He quickly uploaded his speech and handouts to OneNote and assigned tasks to members of his team to help with edits and printing. He even recorded a quick video explaining an important task for his assistant, Dan.

In addition, Harold was using many of the features we had discussed to work smarter and faster. He triggered his Amazing AutoCorrectors, transformed e-mails, did rapid research via his Searchbots, and used his Zipcuts to copy and paste ideas via OneNote. His ZipZone robot helped him find key project documents in a flash. He was clearly amazed at how much more productive he had become.

"What's happening to me?" he asked.

"You're zipping, Harold," I said, wiping a tear from my eye, "and you're morphing."

As he worked, I could see amazing changes occurring to his body. The hair on his arms was slowly disappearing, his

body was growing steadily, and his whiskers where retract-
ing into his face. Suddenly, I realized that Harold was in
full command of his robots. He was even pausing to teach a
tip or two quickly to a team member online.

"I'm so proud of you." I sniffed.

"Thanks, Z," Harold said as he finished up his press
conference preparation. His transformation was now
complete.

He'd morphed from overwhelmed hamster to trium-
phant productivity superhero. All the materials, presenta-
tions, and handouts for his big press conference were in
place.

"The only thing missing from the press conference is
me!" Harold said, looking dejected.

The traffic was at a standstill. We had seven minutes to
go. Harold looked sadly out of the window.

"The Darkonians win again!" he sighed.

TIME MANAGEMENT TIPS

Don't Create a Daily Task List

"I'm not so sure about that," I said, as I paid the taxi driver and pulled Harold out of the cab. "When you become a productivity superhero you get special powers."

With that, I grabbed hold of Harold, pointed my fist at the sky, superhero style, and cried out, "Up, up, and away!"

Unfortunately, absolutely nothing happened.

I must be using the wrong words, I thought.

Harold's eyes brightened. He had an idea.

"What about, zip, zap, zooooooom!"

We both gasped as we blasted off into the sky. We rose up over the skyscrapers and bridges and shot through the air at an incredible speed. Harold began to laugh wildly as he realized that we did have a chance of making the press conference after all.

"Take that, Darkonians!" Harold screamed. The sky suddenly exploded with thunderbolts as the Darkonians launched a final attack with their chaos beam from deep in outer space. We zigged and zagged right past the chaos and then held steady on our target, the city's conference center dome.

I decided to try something. I let go of Harold, and he began to plummet to the ground.

"Help!" he screamed.

"*ZIP!*" I yelled.

Suddenly, he stopped falling and began to rise. He quickly pulled up next to me with a big grin on his face.

"Thanks for the superpowers, Z!" he yelled. "I can see how important tech management is now, but does this mean that time management is completely dead?"

"No," I shouted back over the wind. "But the nature of work is changing, so you have to adapt."

"What time management advice do you have, then?" Harold shouted as a news helicopter zoomed past us. I could see a stunned reporter inside, pointing wildly.

"First, make sure that you aren't so focused on *the process* of time management that you fail to get things done. It's great to get your inbox to zero or to spend twenty minutes a day creating a long task list, but I often see people using these actions as a way to avoid the tough things they have to do. Sometimes making a sales call is harder than processing the latest, low-priority e-mail. So another core *ZIP!* principle is this."

CORE PRINCIPLE #8

Do the Tough Stuff First to Build Momentum.

"Build momentum for all your tasks by knocking down the hard ones first," I continued. "Within a task you can also build momentum by first attacking the fuzziest part of the task, the one that has you worried about getting it done."

Harold nodded as we swerved to miss a flock of ducks.

"This is useful," he yelled over the wind and all the quacking. "Do you create a daily task list with everything you need to get done?"

"Nope," I replied. "For me, it's more efficient to create a *weekly* top-twenty task list that is tied to my big goals for the year. Then, I create very primitive **tough stuff lists** to make the next hour extremely productive. I'm embarrassed to say this, but I just write down three to five actions on a sticky note. Rather than plan the whole day, I plan the next couple hours and work my tail off to get those tasks done."

Harold nodded. "An hourly tough-tasks list sounds smart. I think I'll try that," he said. "When I spent a lot of time creating lists, I noticed that interruptions, fires, or unexpected meetings always wreck my perfect plan."

"Me too," I replied. "Planning is great, but overplanning can lead to paralysis by analysis. But I know my approach won't work for everyone. It depends on what you do and your specific work requirements."

©2012 Getcontrol.net Contact at info@getcontrol.net.

The clouds parted, the warm sun emerged, and the wind quickly dried our rain-soaked clothes. The intense power of *Zip!* was defeating the Darkonian chaos beam.

We were rocketing toward the conference center, and I could sense that hamsters everywhere were reverting back to human form. I closed my eyes for a brief moment and envisioned a world of productivity superheroes excelling at customer service, discovering life-saving cures, and helping to find the bad guys by working better, smarter, and faster. The Darkonians were in full retreat, and we were managing our chaos like *ZIP!* Tip champs.

"Any final words of wisdom?"

"Just this," I said, pointing my finger at a nearby cloud and zipping a chart onto it.

"This is my **Joyful-Useful matrix™**."

"How does it work?" Harold asked.

"Simple. The chart challenges you to create a balance in your work and life between what brings you joy and what makes you useful."

"So should we leave our jobs if we find no joy in them?" Harold asked.

"No. That's a last resort," I said. "The key is to use the chart to ask yourself, *What would make me excited to do my job?* If you lack motivation, ask yourself some important questions. What has changed? How could this job be more enjoyable? What do I love to do most? Can I add some fun element into my next project that would make it more satisfying? What could I do to be more useful? What can I do to get myself into the upper-right corner of the chart?? That's the sweet spot for motivated, happy employees."

Harold looked thoughtful. "And the answers to those questions can help you reshape the way you approach your job and life?"

"Yes. Once joy and usefulness are aligned, you feel happy, energized, and relevant. I think that finding a useful, joyful project or job is rocket fuel for success."

"I'll definitely give it some thought," Harold agreed. "Rolling out a *ZIP!* Tips program would really make me feel both joyful and useful at work."

"I bet it would," I said encouragingly.

We flew on in silence for a moment, and then Harold shouted, "Whoa! We're here!"

THE PAYOFF

Harold and His Robots Save the Day

Harold broke into a run as soon as we landed outside the swanky conference center, and there must have been a dozen shouting reporters and news cameras tracking our every move. Harold's team burst out of the main entrance and ran toward us, relieved and excited.

One of his aides ran up to me. "You're all over the news! You're trending on Twitter and on every news site on the planet!"

Harold raised his hand to quiet everyone down.

"I'll tell you all about it later. For now, let's focus on making this the best press conference in Foster and Schrubb history! Kiran, review the checklist."

A sharp-looking executive turned to the team. She was holding a checklist that had been printed from OneNote.

"Is the speech on the teleprompter?" she asked.

"Check!" Harold's team yelled.

"Handouts distributed?"

"Check!"

"Presentation on the conference center laptop?"

"Check!"

"Press release published via social media?"

"Check!"

"Hooray for the Collaborator!" Harold exclaimed.

"The what?" Kiran asked.

"Never mind—later. Let's rock!"

Harold strode into the conference hall, which was packed with more than 300 reporters, pundits, and high-level executives from his company. He walked confidently to the podium and delivered an amazing speech, considering what he had recently been through.

One of his aides nudged me and pointed to a sharp-looking, grey-haired exec in the back. "That's our CEO, Peg Williams. She's got a ton riding on this product launch."

The CEO looked pensive as Harold approached the lectern. Occasionally she snuck a nervous glance at the crowd. As Harold progressed through his speech, I could see her start to smile, and the smile turned into a big, confident grin during the Q&A session. Harold used his OneNote notes to nail several tricky questions, and the audience was clamoring to learn more about the new Foster and Schrubb app.

I was glad that all of our *ZIP!* Tip antics had not detracted from Harold's shining moment. When the last question was answered and the press conference ended, the CEO rushed over to Harold and gave him a big high five.

I watched from the shadows, beaming like a proud parent on graduation day.

"Perfecto!" she said, laughing.

Harold heaved a big sigh of relief.

"Peg, I'd like to chat with you about my next organizational development initiative," Harold said excitedly. "I think we can boost productivity, performance, and job satisfaction by improving the way we work with our existing technology."

The CEO smiled at Harold and said, "I know, Harold. I saw the news on the web. The board of directors has been badgering me about ways to get more done on a tighter budget. I think you're on to something with *ZIP!* Shoot me a proposal, and I'll take a look."

Harold was whisked away by his team to work on follow-up actions. He turned to wave at me as he left the building. He was smiling from ear to ear.

The reporters and employees trickled out of the conference center, and soon it was just me sitting on the edge of the now-darkened stage and enjoying a quiet moment of reflection.

My communicator buzzed.

"Well? Did you make yourself useful today?"

"Yes, Mom."

"I hope you're not sitting around on your brains. What did you do?"

"Well, today, I helped the people on a planet called Earth."

"Helped them? How?"

"Together, we saved the planet from total chaos and eventual mass destruction."

"Oh, those nasty Darkonians are at it again? Okay, well, I haven't heard from you in a while. Would it kill you to pick up the communicator or pop over to Planet P? But I see you're busy saving planets, Mr. Big Shot. It's all over intergalactic news, by the way. They interrupted my favorite program . . ."

After chatting for a few minutes, I said, "Hey, Mom, I love you. I'm so glad that you and Dad always pushed me to make myself useful. It's so much fun helping others learn to *ZIP!* You're the best."

"Okay, well, don't forget to eat right and get some exercise. No one likes an out-of-shape superhero. Bye now, Zippy. And . . . I love you too."

"Bye, Mom."

"Well," I whispered as I clicked off the communicator, "*that* was a most productive day."

 **CORE PRINCIPLES**

#1 Tech Management Is the Fastest Way to Get More Done.

#2 Activate Your Robots!

#3 The Best *ZIP!* Tips Work Forever and Everywhere.

#4 See One. Do Five. Teach Ten.

#5 Whoever Manages Their Chaos the Best Wins.

#6 Create One-Click Access to What Matters Most.

#7 Optimize Your Home Page for Career Success.

#8 Do the Tough Stuff First to Build Momentum.

Quick Find Guide

ZIP! Tips are all about activating your technology robots. This handy chart will help you zip to instructions for all the *ZIP!* Tips in this book.

ROBOT	ITS JOB
The Amazing AutoCorrector *page 9*	Saves time by typing long, commonly used phrases with a few keystrokes. *Example: Type out your full department name with only two letters.*
The Draftinator *page 19*	Rapidly adds commonly used snippets and passages to save tons of time and improve communication quality. *Example: Quickly insert commonly used, standardized verbiage into letters or e-mails.*
The Transformer *page 25*	Transforms ordinary e-mails into scheduled to-do items, appointments, meetings, contacts, and more. *Example: Drag an e-mail to the calendar to schedule an appointment.*

ROBOT	ITS JOB
The Zip Zone *page 37*	Creates rapid, always-available access to your most important and frequently used documents, folders, applications, and websites. *Example: Quickly open your expense report or access a frequently used website.*
The AutoDialer *page 44*	Saves thousands of taps per year by having the phone dial secondary phone numbers. *Example: Call a conference number with access codes with a single tap on your mobile phone.*
The Amazing Tower of Learning Power *page 49*	Organizes and prioritizes your home page to maximize performance. *Example: Quickly access the top informational blogs and resources in your field of interest— front and center on your device's home page.*
The Searchbot *page 57*	Zips to helpful information in search engines. *Example: Type "United 235" to access flight info.*
The Volume Crusher *page 63*	Conquers e-mail overload by reducing inbox clutter. *Example: Create rules to move less critical e-mails out of your inbox to handle at a later date.*
The ZipCuts *page 66*	Help you work faster by reducing clicks and mental effort required to do your job. *Example: Type* Control + F *to quickly find information.*
The Collaborator *page 71*	Provides a much better way to record meetings and projects in an easily shared digital format. *Example: Collaborate in real time to create a marketing brochure with your team.*

Acknowledgements

I would like to acknowledge the following amazing contributions to this book.

Rachel Metzger—Your incredible editing lifted this project to astounding new heights. Thanks for helping me bring a world of hamsters, superheroes, and robots to life.

Emilie O'Leary—Thanks for suggesting a deadline for this book. That was smart!

Liza Rivera—Your support, sense of humor, and encouragement over the past five years has helped us build an innovative company with a bright future. A million thanks!

D. J. Manuel—Thanks for pushing me to come up with a new word for time management, personal productivity, and the like. The word *ZIP!* is much, much, much more fun!

Steve Piersanti and Jeevan Sivasubramaniam—Thanks for all of your wisdom. I'm so glad to be launching with the best publishing team in the world.

Jon Barb, Pete Weintraub, Charlie Mitchell, Tracey Campbell, and James Chordas—Thanks for keeping a steady stream of zips headed my way!

Vicki Halsey and Tim Burress—I am grateful for everything you've done for me. Thanks for your support in this solo effort and the launching of the Hamster series.

Jeff Burress, John Ireland, Bill Kirwin, Tim Reichert, Doug Cole, Garrett Miller, and especially my dad—thanks for all the wonderful business ideas and advice.

Chris Volpe—Great photos, dude!

Mom and Dad—You know I love you. Thanks for believing in me.

Kristin—Thanks for believing in me. I love you.

Kids—Thanks for reminding me of what matters most. Love you guys!

Mike Song (aka, Z)
CEO, GetControl.net
2013

INDEX

Services Offered

YOUR TEAM NEEDS TO ZIP!

For more than ten years GetControl.net has helped the world's best and brightest teams to *ZIP!* If your goal is to achieve real, measurable, and lasting performance gains, contact us to today to explore a *ZIP!* Tips keynote, training session, or virtual learning experience.

Tell us about your specific needs, goals, culture, and values, and we will customize a high-impact program that takes your people to new heights.

888-340-3598 | Mike@GetControl.net | www.zip-tips.com

About the Author

Mike Song is a sought-after keynote speaker who has helped millions to *ZIP!* via dynamic appearances on *Good Morning America*, CNN, CNBC, and NPR. In addition to *ZIP! Tips*, Mike is the lead author of the best-selling e-mail effectiveness book, *The Hamster Revolution*, which has sold more than 150,000 copies in twelve languages.

Mike has worked with 20 percent of the Fortune 500 including Mercedes, Microsoft, and McDonald's; he has surveyed more than 50,000 professionals and presented to audiences in fifty countries around the world. Mike is CEO of GetControl.net, one of the world's premier productivity training organizations. GetControl.net provides highly effective, compact training modules covering the biggest productivity pain points experienced in today's workplace.

Mike is available for custom-designed training and keynote speaking engagements targeted specifically to help your organization *ZIP!* **For more info: 888-340-3598 or Mike@GetControl.net.**

Also by Mike Song (with Vicki Halsey and Tim Burress)

The Hamster Revolution
How to Manage Your Email Before It Manages You

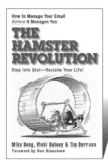

Is email taking over your life? Meet Harold, an HR director so overwhelmed by email that he feels like a hamster on a wheel. Just in time, Harold meets a leading expert on email efficiency and etiquette with a simple system that helps Harold eliminate needless emails, write better messages, and file and find information in a flash. He gets immediate results—and reclaims his life.

Paperback, 144 pages, ISBN 978-1-57675-573-0

PDF ebook, ISBN 978-1-57675-575-4

The Hamster Revolution for Meetings
How to Meet Less and Get More Done

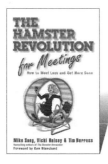

In this book it is Iris, a sales director, who turns into a hamster as she scurries from meeting to meeting. She meets a coach who identifies the five biggest meeting pain points and shows her practical new solutions tailored to our technology-driven world—she discovers how to use e-calendars, PDAs, and virtual meetings to make her life easier, not more complicated.

Hardcover, 168 pages, ISBN 978-1-60509-007-8

PDF ebook, ISBN 978-1-60509-008-5

BK® Berrett–Koehler Publishers, Inc.
San Francisco, www.bkconnection.com   800.929.2929

Berrett–Koehler
Publishers

Berrett-Koehler is an independent publisher dedicated to an ambitious mission: *Creating a World That Works for All*.

We believe that to truly create a better world, action is needed at all levels—individual, organizational, and societal. At the individual level, our publications help people align their lives with their values and with their aspirations for a better world. At the organizational level, our publications promote progressive leadership and management practices, socially responsible approaches to business, and humane and effective organizations. At the societal level, our publications advance social and economic justice, shared prosperity, sustainability, and new solutions to national and global issues.

A major theme of our publications is "Opening Up New Space." Berrett-Koehler titles challenge conventional thinking, introduce new ideas, and foster positive change. Their common quest is changing the underlying beliefs, mindsets, institutions, and structures that keep generating the same cycles of problems, no matter who our leaders are or what improvement programs we adopt.

We strive to practice what we preach—to operate our publishing company in line with the ideas in our books. At the core of our approach is stewardship, which we define as a deep sense of responsibility to administer the company for the benefit of all of our "stakeholder" groups: authors, customers, employees, investors, service providers, and the communities and environment around us.

We are grateful to the thousands of readers, authors, and other friends of the company who consider themselves to be part of the "BK Community." We hope that you, too, will join us in our mission.

A BK Business Book

This book is part of our BK Business series. BK Business titles pioneer new and progressive leadership and management practices in all types of public, private, and nonprofit organizations. They promote socially responsible approaches to business, innovative organizational change methods, and more humane and effective organizations.

Berrett–Koehler
Publishers

A community dedicated to creating
a world that works for all

Visit Our Website: www.bkconnection.com

Read book excerpts, see author videos and Internet movies, read
our authors' blogs, join discussion groups, download book apps, find
out about the BK Affiliate Network, browse subject-area libraries of
books, get special discounts, and more!

Subscribe to Our Free E-Newsletter, the *BK Communiqué*

Be the first to hear about new publications, special discount offers,
exclusive articles, news about bestsellers, and more! Get on the list
for our free e-newsletter by going to **www.bkconnection.com**.

Get Quantity Discounts

Berrett-Koehler books are available at quantity discounts for orders
of ten or more copies. Please call us toll-free at (800) 929-2929 or
email us at bkp.orders@aidcvt.com.

Join the BK Community

BKcommunity.com is a virtual meeting place where people from
around the world can engage with kindred spirits to create a world
that works for all. BKcommunity.com members may create their own
profiles, blog, start and participate in forums and discussion groups,
post photos and videos, answer surveys, announce and register for
upcoming events, and chat with others online in real time. Please join
the conversation!

Certified

Corporation
bcorporation.net